Ol' Slim's Views from the Porch
A Plethora of Punditry, A Wonderment of Wisdom

NEW MEXICO
MAGAZINE

Author: Slim Randles
Illustrations: Grem Lee
Editor: Jon Bowman
Copy Editor: Walter K. Lopez
Book Design & Production: Bette Brodsky
Publisher: Ethel Hess

Library of Congress PCN Number: 2007924811
ISBN: 978-0-937206-93-5
Printed in Canada

Ol' Slim's Views from the Porch
A Plethora of Punditry, A Wonderment of Wisdom

Slim Randles
illustrated by Grem Lee

Table of

Contents

A Brief Note about the Creators

This book of Slim and Grem's will show why these two artists enjoy the outdoors better than the indoors, and appreciate wild and domesticated animals at least as much as they do human beings. In these pages they give some out-loud smiles of recognition as well. Yes, and readers may even find themselves revealed in these so carefully chosen, illustrated adventures.

If ever there were two creators who seem fated for partnership in these off-kilter viewpoints, they are Slim Randles and Grem Lee. Between them they have worked and played in a very wide spectrum of places. They've done their deeds in Alaska and California, New Mexico and elsewhere. Combined, they have been, and probably still are, involved in everything from magazine editing and writing to ranching, cowboying, tomato growing, professional hunting, fishing and guiding, and, of course, there is the mule packing and consequent dude guiding and consoling. Lumping these two talents together gives them acres of reserves to call upon.

While writing contemporary novels set in Alaska and other parts of the American West, Slim's day job was as metro journalist for the *Albuquerque Journal* for more than a decade. This gave him the opportunity to interview a rich variety of characters: old coon hunters, bull riders and assorted celebrities of every attitude.

Grem's original and realistic drawings of ranch and wildlife are hanging in many homes and public places across the Southwest. Although most of his work has a touch of pathos and humor, it was decided that a cartoon style would be the most effective way to illustrate "Ol' Slim's View from the Porch."

Recently, Grem's artistic talent was honored by Sidney Mauldin, brother of former Santa Fe resident Bill Mauldin, who was the most famous of all the World War II cartoonists. Sidney gave all of late brother Bill's art supplies to Grem. He immediately put the precious materials to work. Grem said of the gift, "I was as happy as a stud buzzard. Sidney is a really kindhearted guy. It's too cool."

A sample of the vast range of these columns

can be inhaled in one titled "Benign Neglect (If It's Broke, Don't Fix It)," wherein many truths are stated. "The New Mexico Thingie Axiom: Things in motion tend to get tired, things at rest tend to heal." They go on and reveal what is already known—that many things will repair themselves if left alone. This subtle satire speaks to us all, but here it's applied with a definite chuckle.

Then there is "Varmint Registry." It's about how domestic animals are being registered to an obsessive degree. Slim mentions his long tour of writing, editing and guiding in Alaska. He says here, "When I left for Alaska, a mustang was a horse. When I came back it was a registered shaggy animal born in someone's backyard."

Then there is "Doggie Talk." Here we learn with great good humor how human beings can, with a little effort and a sense of humor, begin to know what the howling, yapping, barking in various tones actually mean.

A few misguided people might think that Slim and Grem make too much fun of Santa Fe—they don't, because they can't. There is simply no way a person can jest too much about a city that is the capital of a state harboring all but one life zone and the roadrunner as its state bird. Santa Fe has more fine artists and galleries to represent it than is decent. What city embraces a museum full of original paintings by what is probably America's best-known female artist? Why little ol' Santa Fe, of course, with its Georgia O'Keeffe Museum.

Who would dare twit a city that is located amidst an almost sacred combination of snow-crowned mountains, high-desert sagebrush, crystal creeks, richly pigmented rock bluffs with blue skies as clear and bright as a tropical sea, and often partitioned with ice cream clouds surging into castles, up and up past the flight of birds?

The capital of New Mexico is also at the very core of Western history, going back hundreds of years to the beginning of our great nation. Who else had the immortal Santa Fe Trail to bring it the world and all it produced? What other city has lured more inhabitants per capita from the painting, sculpting, writing, opera, film, high-tech, Hispanic, cowboy and Indian world than Santa Fe? None. So, in all honor, one must give Slim and Grem great credit for their sometimes hidden smiles and chuckles of restraint at Santa Fe.

Anyway, these two speak to all of us, at one time or another, and gouge our attention into noticing how ridiculous we often are and how surprisingly splendid we can be on rare occasions. They have been accused by a few elitists of being hokey at times. Maybe so, but to the openly enlightened, there is revealed a subtle sophistication in their teasing. Take them with an equally mixed glass of vinegar and sweet red wine.

Slim Randles and Grem Lee have both experienced the "down-in-the-dirt" world at ground level. All this and more are adventures that lead to having necessary fun.

With a glancing look, it might seem that they are enjoying mirth at others' expense. However, in looking a little deeper, one will find they are smiling lopsided at themselves most of all. In the masterfully executed "Waiting for the Nobel," included here, we find Slim uses a little sandpaper to delineate the pretentious, but sprays himself with a touch of battery acid. Grem Lee's illustration gives domestic animals the stage, while he spears Slim and himself with an El Greco-like figure and an exceedingly generous Nobel Prize belt buckle.

New Mexico is a vast, wonderfully varied part of the Great Southwest that Slim and Grem tease so well. However, in any given publication, anyone from anywhere could receive a little jolt of recognition, thereby fulfilling the artistic intent.

By participating with them we all should breathe and smile a little freer. Even old Santa Fe would have to stretch to equal that.

your amigo
el' Max (the mongrel) Evans

Max Evans
Author of *Madam Millie, Bluefeather Fellini, The Rounders* and *The Hi-Lo Country*

Slim and Grem

Photo of Slim by Catherine Arntzen

Slim Randles, 64, has written "Ol' Slim's Views from the Porch," a monthly column for *New Mexico Magazine*, since 2003. He has been a popular newspaper columnist for many years, and his syndicated column "Home Country" can be read in more than 80 newspapers across America. He is also the author of eight books.

A former cowboy, mule packer and hunting guide, Randles was also a long-distance dogsled racer in Alaska. He ran the first Iditarod Trail Sled Dog Race in 1973 and was later a race official for that more-than-thousand-mile trek. He divides his time between a home in Albuquerque and a cabin outside Belén.

Grem Lee, 48, is the illustrator of *New Mexico Magazine's* "Ol' Slim's Views from the Porch." The artist has been drawing ever since he could hold a pencil. He was raised on horseback at the Y Ranch in the rough-and-rocky country of southwestern New Mexico. He is a cowboy, a hunter and a hunting guide himself. Also known by Navajos as the crazy white man— *bilaga'ana diigis*.

Grem continues to draw despite having the crippling disease of MS (multiple sclerosis) ... or BS as his family and friends say.

Today the outlaw might be found somewhere in the same desolate Gila Mountains that Geronimo once prowled. *Quien sabe*?

Photo of Grem by Alex Smith

SPRING

Blowin' in the Wind

It isn't spring until you've seen flying concrete blocks

It isn't truly spring in New Mexico until the neighbor's cinder blocks stop by for a visit.

There are lots of steps you have to go through before that happens, of course.

There are the gentle zephyrs that cruise along the ground, bringing candy bar wrappers across in front of the porch. During an occasional gust, here comes empty cookie bags. Looks like that Simpson kid isn't going to lose weight any time soon.

It takes the spring winds a while to get going. You work up to the big blow gradually. We look forward to the full blast, as it blows away the old and ushers in a new chance for life and renewal. And as spring creeps along, with the sun warming the backs of our necks, we begin thinking of worthwhile things. We begin to get grandiose ideas. As we sip coffee in the sunshine, impossible feats become possible. Possible projects become probable. Probable projects we do before breakfast.

Years fall away. Gray hair we've diligently earned becomes dark once again in our minds. We smile more.

We want to fly the flag every few days. The neighbor's new pups are cuter. We make grand ceremonial bows and sweeps of our hands at four-way stops because we like to see the smiles on the other drivers' faces. We hold doors open for women who are 20 years younger and three times stronger than we are. We start reading the fishing reports, even though we know we can't go for another month or so. But we're planning. We're ready. It's almost spring!

We know it's almost spring because our suicidal apricot tree has already bloomed with the first fair day and has long since frozen again.

We know because our friends move more quickly and speak with active verbs.

It's spring, and that means it's time to plant a tree, buy a farm, build a house, write a book, build a canoe, fix the taillights on the pickup, tie dry flies and have another baby. We burn the weeds along the acequia with our neighbors and fry the weeds off our own lateral ditches. The new neon grass looks greener, coming up through the black ashes, too.

The warmth of our Southwest sun has gotten the blood flowing again, and the wind—the ever-strengthening wind—has keyed up our nervous system until we have to do something or go crazy.

The police tell us there are more fistfights, more wife beatings, more murders when the spring winds blow.

But there are also more weddings, pregnancies and newborn foals in the spring sunshine. We have to accept the bad to enjoy the good.

During this time, the do-it-yourself shows on the public television channel change gears. Spring gives the local craftsmen a new agenda. That television lady from the flatlands of eastern New Mexico now shows us how to sew shirts and jackets with extra large pockets in them. To hold the rocks, of course. Ballast blouses. Anchored A-lines.

The garden expert from northern New Mexico switches from petunias to rock gardens. And he isn't kidding.

New Mexico's horse shows feature more draft horses than jumpers, and the boxing matches at the fairgrounds tend more toward the heavyweights.

The single guys down on the Plaza begin giving more of an eye to the tourist ladies in plus sizes. We all start thinking sturdy, about this time.

But from here on the porch, it isn't really spring until you get the concrete blocks. First the wind brings the papers, then the cast-off shirts, then the horse blankets. When the neighbors' salt blocks and firewood start drifting past the house, we know apple blossoms aren't far behind.

And when the concrete blocks start appearing as though they were meteorites, hey, it's spring in New Mexico.

And then we can have coffee with our neighbors when we return their stuff.

Cowboy Genius

Worldly contributions merit mention

Don't look for this in Webster's, but the real definition of a cowboy is a man who'll walk three miles to catch a horse so he can ride a mile to town. And, as true as this might be, the New Mexico cowboy has still contributed greatly to the worlds of science, art, literature, history, commerce, chivalry, philosophy, geography, ridiculousness and fun.

I know how this must sound, coming as it does about a breed of man who believes the greatest invention in the past 100 years is the air conditioner in his pickup, but facts are facts. The way I see it, from here on the golden rocking throne of philosophy looking way off toward Ladrón Peak, a word or two must be said for the New Mexico cowboy's contributions to humanity. And we'll take the categories one at a time until they're all whipped.

Chivalry—It would be hard to beat the example of Florencio Ortiz, a cowpuncher many years ago for a ranch that comprises most of the belly button of the state. After a long wait, he finally got the mail order slicker delivered to the ranch. He proudly tied that cowboy raincoat behind the cantle of his saddle, and then went on a gather with his *compadres*. He kept telling them about his new slicker, and how dry it would keep him, until his buddies were about to look for a braining rock.

Then it started raining, and those boys were about 10 miles from the truck. Florencio donned his new slicker, but the others had left theirs back home and were sitting horseback, miserably watching their dry amigo. So Florencio took off the new slicker and tied it back of the cantle again. When they asked him why he would forego the comfort of a dry ride, he simply said, "When my friends get wet, I get wet."

Philosophy—My old pard, Rocky Earick, who once rode a horse from the Mexican border to Canada just because he hadn't done it before, came up with a great bit of philosophy once. It was one of those bunkhouse moments, you see, just after the lamp was blown out, and he said, "You know how they're talking about how everybody's polluting the world, and causing wars, and tearing down the woods for firewood and piano boards and all that? I got it figured out. Yep. It's the doctors' fault. See,

them doctors keep us all alive too long. Every time we start to die, there they are, whittling and pilling and all that, and we go home and start another war or something. So we just need to get rid of doctors. Then we'll get back to the right amount of people."

History and science—A northern New Mexico cowboy by the name of George McJunkin became a slam dunk for whipping these two categories in one day back in 1908. It was shortly after the huge flood that almost totally destroyed the town of Folsom, and George and his horse found some bones, uncovered by the flooding. Being a good citizen, he reported his find to the authorities, and this led to the discovery of Folsom Man, at that time the earliest evidence of humans in North America.

Geography—Down at the southern end of the state, a cowboy named Jim White had become obsessed with the bat cave that later became known as Carlsbad Caverns.

He didn't discover it, but he was the guy who kept going deeper and deeper in it, and taking snapshots of the weird formations, and kept writing letters about how beautiful it was, until the government sent a guy to look at it and they made it a national park.

Commerce—The folks down in the Claunch area knew him as Mac, the guy who owned one of the local ranches and was a good hand with a rope.

To the rest of the world, he was Malcolm Baldrige, secretary of commerce for the Reagan Administration from 1981 until his death in 1987.

Art—The numbers of cowboys who successfully picked up a paintbrush and attacked canvas, or carved leather, or welded steel, or pounded shoeing nails into figures, are legion. Several, however, pop to mind. Jake Lovato, of Bernalillo, went from cowboying to welding pipe fence to winning national awards with huge metal sculptures. The late Bob Lee depicted ranches and horses and ranch folks on canvas as well as anyone has ever done it. He was the grandson of Oliver Lee, who at one time owned or controlled more than a million acres of ranchland in New Mexico. Bob's nephew, my own *compadre,* Grem, who illustrates this column, is a fine artist in his own right, and comes from a ranch so far in the boonies near Reserve that the only way to get there is to be born there.

Literature—When a northern New Mexico cowboy becomes a successful artist, what would be more natural than to just drop that and teach himself to be a novelist, so that's what Max Evans did. His first novel, *The Rounders,* amply illustrated just how ridiculous the cowboy life is, and made him a bunch of money, so naturally he didn't write too much about cowboys any more and turned out some of the best literature about the West we've ever seen.

Wanna Dine in Santa Fe

Brush up on your Italian, French

To people who don't live in New Mexico, it won't come as a shock to realize that to live and flourish in the city of Santa Fe, one must be bilingual. That's right. One must speak—or at least be able to pronounce— Italian and French.

Spanish? *No problema.* All you need to know are *comida* (food) and *baño* (bathroom) to get along fine in that language. But without a working knowledge of Italian and French, you'll starve to death in the City Different.

Just take coffee. Santa Fe coffee. They make it in stainless steel boilers and sell it for five bucks a cup. The key to ordering is simple: just point to the menu on the wall. The rule for drinking coffee in Santa Fe is this: If you can pronounce the name of the coffee, you don't want it. Cowboy coffee is out. What you want is java that tastes like it's been filtered through shredded tires to give it that certain *como se llama.* They name these concentrated coffees for dead Italian opera singers.

Not everyone grew up with Italian and French, of course, so here are some Italian lessons.

Pasta means noodles. Pesto is not the nickname of your 4-year-old grandson. It is a gravy made of ground-up alfalfa. And, most importantly, antipasto is not Italian for ant paste.

But it is when dealing with the French language that most of us Westerners need help (and where else would you go to get it?).

The key to gentling French is to grunt a lot and don't pronounce consonants. For example, defying any form of reason, hors d'oeuvres is actually not pronounced "horse doovers." Seriously. The first word is pronounced ore, just like in a gold mine. It's the second one that gets tricky. To pronounce it properly, first say the ore, then pucker up and take a deep breath. Now have your brother punch you in the solar plexus as hard as he can. Ever had the dry heaves? That's the sound you're trying for.

With practice, you too can be successful and get tiny cubes of cheese and salami on toothpicks.

The simplest way to learn French pronunciation is simply to pronounce every fifth letter. For example, this makes *eauocieuxa'horstueoastropuauop* the French word for "catsup." Or you can point at a red bottle on the next table and have your brother hit you again. Both are effective.

This love affair with French food, like catsup, came about back in 1850 when Archbishop Lamy brought a bunch of French priests to New Mexico because the Pope believed the Spanish language wasn't hard enough. With the French food came the French music, epitomized by the work of Saint-Säens, whose name is so hard to pronounce, he had to become popular just so the disc jockeys on the classical music station could practice saying his name. He wrote "Carnival of the Animals." That's really all you need to know about that.

He had to be a tough sumbuck, too. His first name was Camille. To be accepted into polite Santa Fe society, you must learn to pronounce Saint-Säens. It makes saying Beethoven or Smetana seem school-yardish. Find a way to insert the name into conversation at a Santa Fe wine-n-cheeser.

"On an evening such as this," you might say, "One can almost hear the mellifluous striations of the cumquatrains of 'The Carnival of the Animals' by Saint-Säens, wouldn't you say?"

If you end it with a question, it puts the ball back in his court and you can sip the merlot and look wise while he tries to figure out what you just said. Raise an eyebrow while you wait. Big points.

But without the proper pronunciation of Saint-Säens, you can forget it. You'll have to stick to Mozart or Elvis.

And here's how to pronounce it right. Just say to yourself "sad songs." Then pronounce the word "sad" without the d, and "songs" without the n and g. Stick the s on the end, though, kinda like an afterthought.

Let's face it, after Saint-Säens, saying Thiele-mann is a piece of cake.

The secret to ordering anything from a Santa Fe-style French menu is to keep your vowels open for business. They love vowels. Pucker a lot. They do it all the time in Paris, which is why they kiss so much in the movies.

So if you're cruising Santa Fe (please remember, half the streets in Santa Fe are named "Paseo de Peralta" and cross themselves more than Archbishop Lamy) and want to know where all the French stuff is, just read the signs. If the business name ends in "eek," you're in French country, Pard. For example, you'll see a sign saying "Le Squeak" and you'll know right off it's a place to buy food for your pet mice. If it says "boutique," you'll know they sell French riding boots.

If it says "Health Clinique," be careful what you order.

One thing to remember when ordering wine is that a magnum doesn't just mean increased muzzle velocity.

We hope this has been of some help to you. Dining in Santa Fe is fun, really. You can always fall back on English with the waiter if you have to. Most of them have at least a working knowledge of simple English, so don't be afraid.

And please remember that *eau de toilet* smells better than you might think.

Coyotes Everywhere

Critters really don't need any saving

He's always right there, lurking with his cunning grin in the fringes of our Southwest minds, just over the concrete block wall on the desert side, in our early morning hearing. He was here before any of us came, and he'll be here long after we're all gone.

He's a coyote. No, he's Coyote. He's a survivor.

When the last coyote bites the dust, there will be no one left to mourn him, except maybe the final cockroach, because this little wild dog has learned to adapt to almost any conditions the world can throw at him. I've never heard of a Save the Coyote Foundation (although there may be one somewhere), and it doesn't surprise me, even though everything from lemmings to whales seem to have fundraising amigos behind them these days. The truth is, the coyote doesn't need any saving, thank you just the same.

There are coyotes earning a good living in New York City, in the garbage cans of the Hollywood hills, in the jungles of Central America, in the Brooks Range of Alaska and in other states where they've never lived before, like Michigan.

And here at home, there are coyotes doing well … everywhere.

"We have no idea how many coyotes are in New Mexico," says Ken Podborny, biologist for the New Mexico Department of Game and Fish. "We don't count them. But they are everywhere and doing just fine.

"There are coyotes at every elevation in the state and in every possible environment. There are coyotes raising their pups right in the middle of Albuquerque. They are very adaptable and eat whatever's available."

That's the other reason why there may never be a Save the Coyote Foundation; one of their favorite foods is housecat.

"Well," says Ken, "they eat what they can. If they have the choice of a fat housecat or a skinny fast rabbit, they'll take the cat."

It's their adaptability to their surroundings, in fact, and their flexible diet, that has caused them so much grief in the past. When man first brought sheep to New Mexico … fat, slow succulent sheep, it didn't take local coyotes more than about 20

minutes to add this to their buffet. In consequence they've been shot, poisoned, trapped and despised by everyone from cattle ranchers to people with chickens in the backyard.

Back when I was young, stupid and flexible, I tried trapping coyotes. Well … I tried trapping coyote: singular. I read a ton of books on trapping, and talked to old-timers about making coyote sets, and did any number of secret things to sets with material that smelled disgusting, and the upshot of this whole deal was, I trained an entire family of coyotes to be "trapwise." Yep. I was dreaming of catching an adult and having that $3 for the hide, you see, which sounded like more fun than selling *White Cloverine Brand Salve* to my grandmother, and decided that I was born to trap coyotes.

The first day, she came alone and flipped over the traps, ate the bait, and left. The second day, you could see where she'd approached the set, then left, returning later with pups. While the pups sat to one side, she flipped the traps and ate the bait. In the days to come, the entire family would visit the set, and the pups would flip the traps.

Novelist Max Evans used to hunt coyotes with sight hounds. Now this was back before the earth cooled completely, in the northeast part of New Mexico that he dubbed "The Hi-Lo Country" in his many books. But one day, not too long after he returned from World War II, Max saw a coyote pup run back to help its mother fight the hounds, stupidly but valiantly, and the pup, naturally, was killed for its troubles. Max never hunted coyotes again.

"I've had ranchers get angry at me because I can't kill a coyote any more," Max says. "I'll hunt other animals for chile meat, but since that day in the Hi-Lo Country, I can't kill a coyote. It would be committing suicide. At best, I'd be killing my brother."

In many American cultures, Coyote has been the focus of great campfire tales, both true and should-be-true stories, and has become the stuff of legends. Why?

Because this is one animal that is so smart we really can't hurt him much. Give him desert heat, Arctic cold, jungle rain, wet swamps, high-rise apartments. It just doesn't matter.

In fact, the encroachment of people, ironically, has helped his numbers, because we grow food for him.

Maybe that's why we respect him so. He's out there, yipping to his family as we wake in the mornings, and that makes us smile. Here's a wild animal who could be parachuted into any place on earth, and in six months he'd have a family and a new diet.

If only people were that adaptable.

Benign Neglect

If it's broke, don't fix it

Science and technology are wonderful things. They've brought us Monday Night Football, eliminated dang near every disease except the Black Death and even filtered the water from the Jémez Mountains.

Now they've given us the key to success in managing the everyday machinery of life, and they've done all that without even once being mentioned in a scientific journal. Why? Because they didn't even know they had done it.

But that's where you and I come in, trained observers of life that we are. And that's why we now have what shall be called The New Mexico Thingie Axiom: Things in motion tend to get tired, things at rest tend to heal themselves.

This first revealed itself, strangely enough, through one of our more recent technological miracles—the computer. As a man now approaching middle age ("Yeah, Pop, but from which end?"), I have what every guy needs to become a true technogeezer: a teenage daughter. When something goes haywire with the computer, and I have committed a fatal error and am condemned to cyber death, I simply throw myself on the mercy of youth and get out of the way. Then I watch, as in a short burst of keystrokes the capital crime has been expunged from all court records and once again guys with gray beards are safe to check e-mail.

"OK," I tell her. "Now show me what you did to fix that."

"No way," comes the reply. "Job security."

So we are left once again at the mercy of people who six months ago had to be taught how to properly pack a mule. But I made one very keen observation during all of this: Every time she finished up with the keystroke magic, she shut down the whole kaboodle and then started it up again.

And there it was, the key to success. How many times have we simply had to let inanimate objects rest a bit before asking any more from them only to have them respond when the time was right? You bet. Seventeen times or two we've seen it happen. Engine on the pickup floods out in the morning, what happens? Go have another cup of coffee and let the poor thing rest and get its battery and carburetor back to normal rhythm.

Then try again and VROOM!

If you miss an easy throw at a calf down at the roping arena, and the guys are giving you the laugh, you just take that catch rope off and go hang it on the fence for a while. Use your back-up rope for the next couple of calves and be sure to let that first rope see how a real rope is supposed to operate, right? Then when you tie hard and fast and build another loop in the first one, you get a fast swing and a calf every time.

Taillight burned out on the horse trailer? Just let it rest. We know from experience that it needs to rest until a police officer brings the situation to our attention.

Radio running out of batteries? Rest that thing for a while and you'll get at least half a song out of it before it goes dead again. Rest. Allowing the self-healing properties of inanimate objects to do their thing. Sleep, Shakespeare said, is the penicillin of machinery, and ravels up the nits of care. That's the key. Rest that thingie and let the little fibrous molecules have a time-out to think about things. Then they'll realize that (1.) There's more pride in doing a job properly, and (2.) They'll appreciate the care you show them in allowing them to rest up a while.

And now that our scientific minds have stumbled on the secret of inanimate complicity, it's time we tested our theory on more objects in our everyday life.

You just take that barbed-wire fence out there. Oh, I could always go out and hook a come-along to it and stretch it tight to keep that mule out of the neighbor's field, but who knows what resentment might build up in those gently oxidizing strands? The fence has been sagging for three years now, but I have faith in science. If I just rest that baby another year or two, no telling how horse-high, hog-tight and bull-strong that thing might become. Maybe I should apply for a research grant.

Once again, science triumphs over the tundra.

Swatting Flies
Early killing spree key to eradication

You can look it up in the almanac. It's right there near "Plant potatoes in the bowels," which sounds painful and disgusting, and "Hunger is the best pickle."

It's the phrase "Kill one fly in May and keep thousands away."

It must be true, because our ancestors said it hundreds of years ago, and they all managed to pass away successfully, so we should pay heed, just as we would a cover charge.

The idea behind this, naturally, is that flies begin emerging from their eggs in the warm air of spring, and each time we bump one off, we prevent them from multiplying and taking over the garbage can. Last year (being of a scientific mind, of course) I personally went on a killing spree and in one day in May kept hundreds of thousands of flies away. The problem was, I couldn't tell the difference. One day in July, I glanced down at my coffee cup, out on the patio, and there was one I'd missed, happily dog paddling through my Coffee-Mate. Obviously, my spring massacre had missed his ancestors somehow.

"If only," I shouted, waving a fist at the universe, "I could coordinate the effort and get everyone to kill a fly in May!"

Once upon a time I was married to a very fine lady near the city of Los Angeles. She was tall and fair, and she knew … knew … that a totalitarian government was the healthiest possible situation for anyone to be in. I have never felt that way, and might have mentioned it to her at the time. Her reply was, "There are no flies in China!"

What?

"Yes," she said, smugly. "No flies. Not a one. That's why the people of China are free of disease." They are?

"Of course. Do you know how many people live in China? A lot. And that's because there are no flies to make them sick."

So how did China become fly-free?

"That's simple," she said, folding her arms and grinning. "The government told the people to swat flies. So they all swatted flies and killed them all. We could do the same thing here, only you can't get everyone to obey the law. It isn't like it is over there."

I'm sure that's true.

Now this statement of hers has bothered me during all the long years since our divorce (there was a little matter of incompatibility there, you see). I kept wondering how there could be no flies in China.

If this were true, this would also mean there would have to be some kind of permanent fly obliteration squad around China's monstrous border. It's one thing for the Chinese to get together and whap the crud out of all its flies, but that doesn't necessarily prevent Mongolian flies or Kazahkstani flies from buzzing across the border. So there would have to be Chinese armed with swatters standing by at the border to prevent flies from reinfesting the healthy and prosperous People's Republic.

Then the following story appeared from Guangzhou, China.

> Employees at a supermarket chain in southern China have been swatting flies—but not because business is bad.
>
> On top of their sales targets, employees at the chain in Guangzhou also have to meet the "flies quota."
>
> At the end of each working day, they have to hand over a specific number of houseflies to their managers as part of the chain's effort to get rid of the pests and keep the stores clean.
>
> At one branch, the male employees had to submit eight houseflies each day while their female colleagues had to meet a quota of five.

Hot dog!

According to this story, not only are there flies in China, but there are obviously too many flies in China, and there are even flies inside the supermarkets in China. On top of that, at least one supermarket chain in the world recognizes that men are better hunters than women, otherwise why the discrepancy in the number of dead flies to be presented (with a bow, no doubt) to the manager? This could also lead to a new form of courting. If a man is a really great hunter, he could get his eight flies and some of her flies for her, too. Throughout history, pretty girls have been attracted to good hunters.

Buoyed by this affirmation in the ultimate superiority of free choice over printed supermarket rules, I shall again this month devote at least 10 minutes of my time to keeping thousands of flies away for later coffee-drinking comfort.

And, if no one else cares to join me in this frenzied insecticide, so be it. Sometimes it's better to live with flies than with rules.

SUMMER

Cool, Enchanted Evenings

The payoff for unbearable daytime heat

It is the heat that defines us this time of year. Defines our sweaty days with the brassy skies and afternoons that make us clamor for shade. The heat gives us an excuse to make June the biggest beer-drinking month of the year and returns certain words to our vocabularies. Cooler pads. Swampers. Squirrel cages.

The days themselves aren't much fun, and we pity those who spend the days working outdoors, even as we envied them in the soft warmth of spring. The heat is an entity now, an oppressive, overbearing beast that weighs on our brains and taxes our bodies.

It's the desert tax. The price we pay each summer for living in such a beautiful place.

But there is a payoff.

When the sun goes down, it's romantic enough to hug a cactus.

The recipe is simple. Keep the earth warm, but just bring out the stars and a soft breeze that cools the skin. Mix this with a fulmination of little night varmint sounds of peeping and chirping and croaking. And guitars. Whether we play them ourselves or just turn on the radio, it is a setting perfect for guitars. Villalobos, Fernando Sor, Tarrega, Randy Travis, Doc Watson.

We sit in brick-paved patios with something cool and someone sweet and relax and talk about dreams, because on evenings like this, anything is possible. On nights like this, it's difficult to decide whether remembering evenings like this in the past is better than thinking of more to come. All we really know is that it sure is nice to be here right now.

A high desert evening is a testament to the good things of life. Iced tea tastes better, showers feel more refreshing, neighbors seem nicer. There they are, out on the porch with all the kids. Ah, those wonderful kids … well, yes, they're the same ones we complained about in March, but on a night like this… all is forgiven. Let's wave back.

Rudolph Valentino became a romantic idol to our great grandmothers not because he was particularly handsome or had a good pick-up line. They couldn't talk in those days, of course, and about all he could do in a silent movie was twitch his eyebrow and wear bathrobes. Any guy can teach himself to do that. No, what the sheik had going for him was that he rode a good horse and lived in a tent in the desert. If a guy has a good horse and a tent, and puts them both in a summer's evening in desert country, he becomes an instant chick magnet. Try it. I've heard it's more effective than a six pack and a conversion van.

The trick is to magnetize the right person, of course.

Some say winter snowstorms are the time for reflection on past sins and triumphs, and they make a good point. But a summer evening, with a slight breeze kissing the skin, some lemon in the iced tea, and someone to smile at you—pretty tough to beat that. And the real beauty of it is that the weather is so nice you want to go walking and visiting and laughing.

Everything is a matter of comparison. Boy is it hot here, right? Well, just during the day. Have you ever been through the Needles, Calif., fruit station at 1 a.m. in June? Hundred and six. Things aren't bad here at all.

And you can hear that bank of baby trees along the concrete block wall, sending out more roots and growing those leaves bigger for the heat of the day to come tomorrow. Wonder if there's time to plant even more of those before the rains come. I believe I'll try that. Tomorrow. Early. Before it gets too hot.

Tonight I'm going to see if I can remember all the words to "Little Joe the Wrangler" and find out if my guitar is still in tune.

Varmint Registry

If it's brown, come on down

One of the good things about sitting out here on a sunny day is that you get really smart after drinking a few cups of coffee and giving the hound a few ear rumples.

I think I've finally found a way to pay for the groceries. The plan revolves around animals and the people who love them. Great animals. The best animals. I mean registered animals, of course.

I first noticed the registry revolution when I returned from some really cold terrain to the sunny Southwest. There were few horses in Alaska, and the ones there were pretty hairy. No one cared much about a pedigree as long as that thing didn't eat too much expensive hay, had legs long enough to walk in the snow and could whip a bear.

But down here in sunshine country, where horses are treasured, a registered horse was cherished far beyond any steed in the world. It meant that horse's ancestry was proven and that you could take him to a horse show and pay entry fees. There were purebred quarter horses, thoroughbreds, Arabians and appaloosas when I left. It's hard to describe the heartbreak a teenage calf roper feels when he has to admit to another cowboy that the pedigree of his beloved $50 horse is really by freight train out of Utah.

But when I returned, there were all kinds of new registries of horses I never knew existed. Coming back to horse country, I was met with registered breeds like Trakhener, Bashkir Curlies, Peruvian pasos, Ponies of the Americas, and Holsteiners (which I incorrectly thought would be used to herd milk cows).

When I left, a mustang was a wild horse. When I came back, it was a registered shaggy animal born in someone's backyard. A mule can now be a registered mule, even though its parents aren't, by definition. A mule is either a mule or it isn't—papers won't change that—but there is a mule registry.

But the real eye opener was when people began registering horses that were only half of a breed. This found its societal zenith when some genius founded the Half-Arab Registry. No one takes themselves and their horses more seriously than the folks who own Arabs, and this way some

people could take themselves at least half that seriously. The new breed didn't much care what the other half was, just as long as one half of that horse had large nostrils, soft hooves and could snort.

For years now, Albuquerque has been an every-other-year site for the National Arabian and Half-Arabian Horse Show. A few years ago, some guy showed up with two genuine registered half-Arabs and beat the pants off his competitors in the cowhorse competition. The only problem was, his half-Arabs were half donkey, making them half-Arab but full mules. Having a set of long ears on a dished face sent the purists into screaming terwilligers and inoperable facial twitching. During an emergency meeting of the board of directors, the half-Arab folks changed the rules. They still don't care what the other half is, as long as it is horse.

So this is my third-cup-of-coffee-on-the-porch plan. I hereby announce the founding of the American Brown Animal Registry. Do you have a brown dog, cat, finch? Send me 10 bucks and a certificate of authenticity will wing its way to your home … eventually. Horse, cow, sheep, pig, turtle? As long as it's brown, you're in. Goldfish has a brownish tinge? Hang Bubbles' papers behind the aquarium for the world to see.

Now we're not insensitive to folks whose varmints are tonally challenged. If your animal isn't brown, that doesn't exclude it from the American Brown Animal Registry.

For a special consideration (let's call it an additional 10 bucks, shall we?) your treasured animal can receive a special certificate with a color exemption, a hue dispensation, as it were. We'd hate to see anyone tolerate living with an unpapered mongrel, after all.

Imagine the prestige. For a mere $20 —a small portion of your monthly bar bill—your old white cat could be a registered American Brown Animal. Now there's no reason to hang your head when someone asks if your pet is registered. And you can take heart, knowing the free enterprise system is alive and healthy on at least one New Mexico porch, and that you have helped feed my registered brown mule and registered brown hound, too.

Mystery of the Orphan Shoes

There has to be a rational reason for roadkill footwear

Well, sir, there it was, kinda cramped looking, between some four-wing saltbush and an empty six-pack ring alongside the highway.

I think they call them "Mary Janes," that particular kind of woman's shoe. Size 6, maybe a fat 5.

Been there quite a while at this point. All that raven's wing, plastic fantastic gloss gone out of it by this time, of course. Now it was just a dead shoe, sitting in the purgatory of a New Mexico bar ditch waiting for the highway department or a starving coyote to determine its ultimate resting place.

It was the left shoe. A fairly thorough search failed to turn up the shoe's mate. Of course, that wasn't surprising, because most roadkill shoes tend to be loners.

Not always, however. Daughter Youngest—to promote domestic tranquility let's make that Beautiful Daughter Youngest—starts young horses on the road to civility and social grace as part of her life. She was squiring a young filly down a dry arroyo last winter and came across seven shoes, lined up, a long way from anything we'd call a road. Two of the seven shoes matched.

It is enough of a mystery for inquiring minds to try to figure why one shoe would be alongside a road without a mate. To have five orphan shoes sitting alongside a matched pair is a diamond-studded puzzler.

There are several theories we kicked around over a pot or two of coffee recently. Single shoe theories and multishoe theories.

Possible Orphan Footwear Scenario No. 1—"OK, you kids, I'm telling you for the last time. If there's any more fighting back there, I'm going to pull this car over, take off one of your shoes and throw it away. Then one of you will just have to spend the afternoon at Grandma's hopping around on one foot, looking ridiculous."

Possible Orphan Footwear Scenario No. 2—"Well, I know you say you love me, Pamela Sue, but how can I be sure? Talk is cheap, but love and trust should last a lifetime. I'm willing to drive in from the ranch each Saturday night to see you, but what kind of sacrifice have you made to show me you're serious?

"What are you doing? Say, isn't that your brand-new Mary Jane, all shiny with raven's wing gloss? And you're tossing it out into the desert night just for me?

"Aw Honey ... I don't know what to say. No girl's ever done anything like that for me before. Do you like big weddings?"

But things get more complicated when we consider the plight of the Mysterious Arroyo Seven.

Possible Multifootwear Scenario No. 1—"Look, guys, we're lost out here in the desert without a clue as to where we are. The lights from Albuquerque over there aren't really bright enough to show us how to get back to civilization. Before long, maybe a week or two, we'll die of thirst or something. As your leader, I know the only chance we have is to lighten our burdens. I'll set the example by removing both my shoes to save weight. The least you can do is take one of yours off to make travel easier."

Possible Multifootwear Scenario No. 2—"I've brought you out here where there's some privacy kids, so I can teach you how to dance without the possible embarrassment of having your friends see you through the window. It's the least a father can do for his kids. I want to be proud of you at the sock hop next week.

"OK, first thing you do is take off your shoes.

"There's mine. No ... BOTH of them. ..."

But it's the lonely single shoes that tug at our hearts. Even rattlesnakes have mates.

Maybe someone with loose shoes was doing the Hokey Pokey out here.

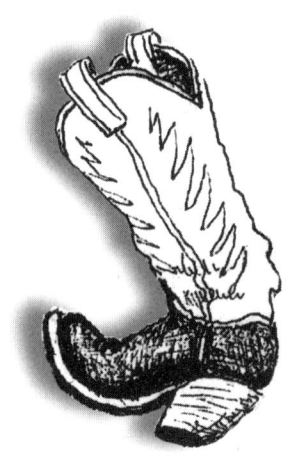

Doggie Talk

Bawls and barks a language of their own

You don't learn the language of dogs overnight. It's an acquired skill, brought about by years of buying dog food and watching it transmogrify into unusable compost.

That wasn't always my view, however. Back before the earth cooled completely, I was a college student with a flattop haircut and a 45 rpm record of Jim Reeves singing "Cattle Call." I was the coming generation. I could do the Babcock test for butterfat in milk down at the ag school. I was right on the verge of knowing everything. I was hot stuff.

Therefore I was dismayed when I first got kidnapped by old-timers to go coonhunting with a pack of hounds.

For the benefit of the uninitiated, what happens is you turn a bunch of dogs out of the back of a pickup truck and wait while they run all over the mountain range, sniffing things. If one of the dogs should sniff something interesting, such as the trail of a raccoon, that dog will "open"—which means bawl his brains out telling the others they are stupid, and he found the trail first.

Then the others have a race to see who can get to the track second, so as not to appear as backward as the dog who comes in third.

Over farm and fen and frogs they run, singing to the night (it's night because 'coons are nocturnal) until finally the raccoon gets tired of the noise on his back trail and climbs a tree to get away from the racket.

Then we tell the dogs they did wonderfully and drag their unwilling butts back to the truck to try for yet another noisy-night triumph.

That's how it happens, but that isn't the real thrill of it. Nope. For the hunters, it is being able to sit on the tailgate of the truck and do the play-by-play announcing of the chase. That's because it's all about the way the dogs hunt and not about the 'coon at all.

"Looks like Baldy's catching up," Jim said. "He's gaining on Dummy. Just listen to that!"

"He ain't gaining on my Dummy at all," Joe said.

"That's just 'cause they hit that arroyo and the bawling sounds farther away when the dog's down in the bottom. See? Hear him now? Heck, he's a

good 50 yards ahead of your dog."

All this is deduced, mind you, from the far-off babbling of dog voices. About the most a neophyte 'coon hunter can tell about it is that the dogs are over that way somewhere.

That's why I was chuckling to myself that first night. How dumb do those old-timers think I am? Hey, I'm a college student, for crying out loud.

Fast forward through about a hundred tons of dog food, running the Iditarod Trail Sled Dog Race with huskies, and treeing mountain lions, bears and about a dozen raccoons with hounds—over and over again. Fast forward through dating and marriage to fatherhood and grandfatherhood and divorce and a beard that turned mysteriously gray when I wasn't paying attention.

Now, out in the woods, the language is clear. For example, if my Molly is hunting a certain stretch of the Río Grande and opens on a track frantically, what she's saying is this: "Hey! It's the Ghost Coon of Tomé! I'll get that sorry sapsucker this time! Even if he swims the river again, I'll go get him."

The young kids with me just think there's a dog bawling down in the bosque, because they haven't bought enough dog food yet. But there is the beautiful language of the night, dear ol' Molly off down there in the trees chasing the Ghost Coon of Tomé.

Now when we start home tonight, and are driving past that ranch up there, listen carefully, and you can hear plainly what Molly is saying to those noisy ranch dogs.

"Oh yeah? Well, who's riding in the truck and who has to run around on the ground tonight? That's right, you ground-hugging, sheep-chasing idiots. You're just jealous, because I'm a hound and that's something you can never hope to attain.

"I tree 'coons and lions and bears and you are just a yapping little mutt trying to guard a driveway!"

But it's on the trail where you can really tell the story. Yep. Sitting there on the tailgate…

"Well, looks like Molly's catching up to Boone."

"Not a chance. He's getting farther ahead."

"Betcha an iced tea she's first to the tree."

"You're on."

And the amazing thing is, from right there on the tailgate, we'll both know what happens.

It has something to do with the night, and the moon, and good friends and good dogs. And buying uncounted tons of dog food while our beards turned gray.

Soaking Up Summer

Quenching rain is nature's treasure

When the world is hot and my skin is fried, scratching from the constant dry, let the clouds boil up—boil up high. And then shade the Earth with the darkening sky and bring the secrets and the smell of rain. The heat and the blessed rain, again.

Our land is brown but blessed, stressed in the heat, the shiny heat of day. The slender green of rivers slides along, striving to continue, to feed its own along the banks—the banks where the dust rises. Rises, powdery clomp by clomp as we walk—walk the shady way.

And though the heat, the dryness of heat, pushes down our weary feet, we plod along. Ours is the blessing of challenge, to live, to thrive in the heat.

To toil and sweat, to make the cold drink at day's end that much sweeter. Sweeter as it goes down, cooler as it falls, dropping the coolness inside us and forcing us to smile. That summer smile. We begin to grin and know, as shades of evening droop on the western hills, that we did it once again. We were measured and we did it. Did it with our hands, today. Did it in the heat, today.

Did it when we were tired, today. We are here, we have worked, the bread is ours, the sweeter, the heavier for the toil, for the heat.

When the heat falls hard, on many days, unquenched by the dark of night, we ask—in quiet times—we ask. Bring us the clouds, the black-bellied clouds, the clouds that softly hold the heads of gods in their moistening grasp.

The clouds, those big-bellied busters that hold the violence, the wind, the flashes, the noise. The clouds we wait for and pray for and look for on the western ridge. Let them come, with their silver tops and their bellies black as night and cool as forgiveness.

The summer clouds, the clouds that define our culture, our art, our summer, our hot, heavy summer. The clouds, the rain, the respite from the toil. To soak the thirsty soil. Bring the listening to the tin roofs as the clouds beat a tattoo for us.

Let the magic come and stay, stay for a while, at least for a while, and wet us down, all the way down. Fill our pores, smooth our skin, wash us free of dirt and sin, with the rain, the cleansing, blessing rain.

Sink the water to the core of the earth and push it through the dust, making it heavy and loath to leave the ground.

Bring the smells, too, of life, and water, and the heat and the cooling and friends and dogs that are wet and happy. Waggily happy, stick-biting happy, rolling in temporary mud happy, laughing with tongues no longer parched.

When it's done, when it's over, when we've had our treasure and the clouds have gone to feed the plains, please, a rainbow. An arch of treasure and triumph and farewell and pleasure until the passion of the heat brings us yet another day like this.

Another day of clouds, of life, of rain, of supreme love and comfort, of one more treat for man and his animal friends. Another day. Wait until it's right, but then, another day, please.

Bring the big rollers in from the west, and let us watch the world get its fiery drink, and drink in the noise and think about cooler times, but know…let us know that there is nothing better than this.

A rain, a storm, a suddenness of life and blast and sweet charity designed to keep us living here, here in the rain, here in the sun, and keep us praying, here in the rain, and looking toward the west for more, always to the west, always looking for more.

The Best or Nothing

Being close just doesn't cut it

There is no glory in almost.

When the judge of the New Mexico Cowboy Dutch Oven Cookoff came over to me after the event with an apologetic look on his face, I braced myself. Oh, I knew my longtime rival had won the thing, as he'd already received his honors, and I hadn't.

"Pardner," the judge said, "I gotta tell you, that cobbler of yours was great stuff. Really. It was a close thing between your cobbler and the winner's."

His face kinda scrunched up then and he held fingers up as if to pluck an answer from the ether. "Your cobbler ... your wonderful peach, pineapple and sourdough cobbler was great, but it just didn't have that little extra ... *como se llama* ... know what I mean? It missed, but just by this much."

And the winning cobbler? What was the extra little something it had?

"Brandy," he whispered.

I felt just like the guy who invented WD39. Never heard of WD39? No one has. There had to be one, though. We know the company came up with WD40 and stopped right there.

"We love your WD39 formula, pardner," the chairman of the board probably said, "I mean, that stuff coats unmoving objects, it repels water, it makes doors swing silently on happy hinges. It's just wonderful.

"But you see ... WD40 does all of those things, too. And a little extra ... something besides. WD40 takes shoe stains off linoleum."

Coming in second is the pits.

Maybe it's a good time to consider the people who almost, but not quite, made history and became rich beyond their wildest dreams of avarice.

Have you ever heard of 999 Island Salad Dressing? Of course not. There would have to be that other guy who stuck another kumquat or something into his blend to come up with Thousand Island.

It couldn't have been any fun to slave away to get a college degree in chemistry, then work in a dark laboratory for 30 years only to come up with Formula 408, either.

Ever meet a woman who was proud of dabbing a little Chanel No. 4 behind her ear? I think not.

And the world of sports has had its losers, too.

RUBEN'S 30 FLAVORS OF ICE CREAM

Bean Dip Flip	Heart Burn Habanero	Mint Menudo
Chili Con Queso	Vanilla Vinegerone	Cherry Chorizo
Pinto Bean Praline	Relleño Royale	Mescal Whirly Worm
Tamale Tart	Chili Chip Crunch	Huevos Rancheros
Chicharoni Sundae	Pastacio Picante	Enchilada Eclair
Fudge Frijole	Pico de Gallo	Tequila Swizzel
Taquito Tangerine	Turtle Tripa	Choco Cucaracha
Grasshopper Gordito	Lizzard Lengua	Poco Loco Burro Joe
Salsa Santa Fe	Jalapeño Hazelnut	Señorita Margarita
Prarie Dog Pecan	Frito Bandito Pie	Fajita Bonita Chiquita

Shakes and Floats
Red or Green
Hot or Mild
$1.00

New!
Green Chili Cheese
Sandwiches
$1.50

All Flavors .50¢
Blue Corn Tortilla
Ice Cream Cones
.25¢

This is not just limited to athletes, but to the promoters and designers of famous sports events.

For example, can you name the guy who first tried to produce the Indianapolis 499? Not likely. How about horse racing's Double Crown? That poor guy will remain unsung, I'm afraid.

College basketball's Final Three? The World (except for parts of Myanmar) Series?

There are tears there, a trail of pain and defeat. Talented people, without doubt, but at the closing, failed to make that stretch run into history and fame.

How would you have liked being the automotive engineer who went to Henry Ford with your plans for the Model S? Or if you concocted the barbershop trio? The Chicago Six?

At Boeing, it must have been heartbreaking that day when the designer was called in.

"Pardner," they probably told him, "We loved your design, and I must say your Boeing 746 is an engineering marvel. The idea that you can get 399 people off the ground in one airplane is just stunning. But we're going to have to go with this Boeing 747 design because it holds an even 400 people.

"You see, this new design has a place for the pilot to sit, too."

I'll bet Alaska barely had time to have the tourist brochures printed, telling everyone they were welcome in "The Land of 9,999 Lakes" when Minnesota did what they did. Alaska had to settle for "The Great Land" instead. Sounds good, I guess, but will it play with fishermen?

What if Heinz had only 56 varieties? What if the one they forgot was ketchup?

It's aggravating enough to make you wish you drove a three-wheel-drive vehicle just to honor that earlier inventor.

The only redeemable fact of this whole mess is the certainty that one day there will be a WD41. This one will lubricate, clean scuff marks and will have that little extra *como se llama*. It will cure saddle sores, too. Then the guy who came up with WD40 will know what it feels like to just slightly miss the mark.

It's still tragically true. Close only counts in horseshoes and hand grenades.

FALL

A Summer Respite

Fine tuning yourself can be refreshing

When the first wisps of cool brush my home in early morning, let me go to the high country.

As the valley bakes to a bronze finish in the late summer sun, let me walk where eagles fly on silent deadly searches. Take me up to the cool shade of the evergreens, let me hear the bugling of the elk, the hunting cry of the coyote.

Let me cry a little hunter's cry, too.

For it is the time of polishing, of refining, of brushing to a slick gloss all the traits that make us the most complicated of animals. It is the mating time, the hunting time. It is the time of golden leaves and soft ground that sinks softly as we step upon it. It is the time of being alert and looking around us and trying the ages-old instincts once again.

It is the time of perfection, that time when the antlers are sharpest, coats are shiniest, teeth are whitest and eyes see things that may or may not be there.

Let me go to the high country, greet the timberline, slip in and out of the trees, walk the open spaces high above the Dutch oven valleys below.

Let me try once more to be the best I can be, to savor life, to sip once again that coffee from the fire, straight as life itself. And though there's no sugar or cream, we know it's the best we'll ever have.

Tell me stories, there by the fire, as we keep our traditions alive with color and beauty and the breathless parts of terror. Let me remember your face as it looks in firelight and please remember me that way. Let the stories come, polished or plain, true or should-be true. This is our way to be humans, to keep going, to let young people know this is how we are and who we are.

Because we know, at life's slowing, that the most important thing we did was to make memories with others.

When we walk the high country, the tall highups where no motors go, we drink in the quiet like soft wine on a fancy picnic. For a while—a golden special while—we are above everything but life itself. The world may not be ours, but for a while, we are not the world's either. Down in the noise people worry and take pills and look at their watches. For a while, though, we look up only to see clouds and answers.

The world may not be mine, but I am not the world's either, for this moment in time, and that time will stay with me through the cold months of winter, the winds of spring and next summer's frantic heat. This time of beauty and peace and prayer is my time, and your time, and the high country is home. It is our old home. The old home place we remember only when we are alone and quiet and in that magic time between sleep and morning. In our old home, each canyon is a room, each tree an umbrella, each animal a kindred spirit. And while there, we hear the music of the mountains and the mind. We see the laughing faces of those who are now in far distant camps and will never be in this camp again. We see things and hear things we don't mention to others because to do so would profane the perfection of memory.

And when we're there, we'll immerse our-selves in the cleansing bath of air that smells of the perfume of life itself, and be thankful.

Too soon our rooms will be smaller and less beautiful. Too quickly our minds will work on small problems again. But this is our moment, high up here where no one goes except those who would be our brothers and sisters. This is our time. Our moment. We, too, become perfect, even if just for an instant. But that is enough. We know, through the cold and clutter of winter, that we had our perfect moment and we will keep that inside, like a shiny rock in a special pocket. And we'll know.

And if we sing a heart song as we look across the mountains, let us be forgiven if it isn't perfect yet.

Because inside we know it's meant to be perfect, and the mountains are kind enough not to tell.

Then, when the heart is full, we can go back down the mountain as new souls, full of kindness, and we can each work to find a mate and a place out of the cold to come.

The Blessed Bean

There's nothing on earth like coffee

As a recycled cowboy, it gripes me to have to realize that for much of my happiness I am indebted to hyperactive sheep.

According to legend, sheep who were grazing in what is now Ethiopia started munching red berries—about A.D. 1000—and started frisking about and having fun.

The sheepherder, named Kaldi, chewed some of these berries, grinned, and said, "Man, I just can't live without my coffee."

Which just goes to show that some things never change.

Coffee, of course, is one of the world's three basic food groups, the other two being barbecue potato chips and corn dogs. Coffee has become so important in our daily lives that the entire Pacific Northwest has come down with a gang addiction. On a recent trip to Oregon, I noticed that every two blocks in all the bigger towns there were drive-up coffee kiosks where you are able to pay $4 for a cup of coffee that tastes like it was filtered through shredded tires and whose name is unpronounceable.

And about the time the breakfast coffee rush wore down (shortly after 2 p.m.) a distinctly Pacific Northwest ritual began, known as "the afternoon perk."

Here came the long lines of cars again, with hands grasping $5 bills reaching out the car windows and shaking with the early stages of withdrawal.

Ahh, the bean, the blessed bean. Oh bean, thou art craved in the deepest fibers of our being, thou infiltratest our cellular essence with the sunshine of morning and brusheth away the cobwebs of gloom.

Back when I was guiding hunters, I had one German industrialist who couldn't stand the way we made coffee. One morning in the tent, ol' Wilhelm said, "You Americans know nothing about coffee ... get out of my vay!"

Wilhelm then filled a pot with water, threw in what appeared to be an equal amount of coffee and fended me off with a three-tined fork until this mess had boiled for about 10 minutes. I watched carefully, and my notes tell me that German coffee is done when the white speckles melt off the enamelware pot.

"Dis," pronounced Wilhelm, waving his arms as his eyes flew open, "is COFFEE! Vun cup, you are good for a veek!"

It was strong, all right. We hunted 75 hours straight and had a footrace back to the coffeepot when we finished.

On our ranches we have many different rules. Some ranches don't allow photography, some welcome fishermen, some shun outsiders who want to hunt. But all of them have one inviolate rule: The coffee must go on. There is somewhere a pot of coffee in the house, and if it is empty, it is filled again immediately whether there is anyone there to drink it or not.

Friend or foe, process server or godfather, Scylla or Charybdis, it matters not. All are welcome at the caffeinated fount of New Mexico hospitality. You wouldn't even shoot a guy for dumping your daughter without giving him a cup of coffee first.

Coffee was even given a papal blessing back in 1600, you know. There were a bunch of Christians (obviously on decaf) who were petitioning Pope Clement VIII to ban coffee for being the devil's drink. He didn't want to do that without trying it first, being a fair-minded kinda guy, so he had some cardinal whip up a batch and he sucked it down. He gave the drink his blessing, said it was an official Christian beverage, had a mug made with "Clem" on it and hung it over the sink.

There is nothing on earth like coffee. It gets into the very marrow of our bones and makes us live long and happy and energetic lives.

Decaf, you say? (Decaf should be made legal grounds for divorce.)

Tea? (Point to the globe and show me what's left of the British Empire. 'Nuf said.)

Of course, you can take coffee ingestion to a ridiculous degree. Does the term "blitzkrieg" paint a picture? But for most of us, we take it black, we take it with cream and sugar, we take it any way we can get it, but we take it.

It's kept some people moving and writing columns years after they were declared literarily brain dead.

Long live nervous Ethiopian sheep. Please pass the sugar.

Holing Up

Want ads hold the key

There's nothing wrong with a regular home. It can be fun to have a hot shower and watch TV every now and then. It's just that a guy needs a hole-up spot of his own.

You know what a hole-up spot is. That's the kind of place where a guy can hole up and do things.

"Yep, he's holed up writing a book," or "I'm going to hole up and spend some time with those colts."

That's a hole-up spot.

Now it doesn't have to have running water or electricity. Those things aren't important with a hole-up spot. But it has to be kind of away, you know. In a nice place.

But a good hole-up spot isn't easy to locate. In the first place, one must usually deal with real estate folks, who are the attack dogs of New Mexico commerce. They discovered this state has only 121,365 square miles of land, and they have to hurry before someone else sells it. And they sniff at the thought of hole-up spots. Some even snort at the thought. That's because a hole-up spot doesn't have to be expensive. To a real estate piranha, that

means small commissions. But they'll never take us alive, because that means there are 77,673,600 acres in this beautiful state, (amounting to about 52 acres per resident) so there should be at least one that is right for holing up.

So we turn to the want ads. But the ads, it turns out, are the last legal place where lying is not only allowed, but encouraged.

So I read, I called up, and I went to see land. Hey, all I wanted was a little place where I could throw up a cabin and no one could toss me off, you know? Typewriter, hounds, my old mule, Jack, a Dutch oven or two. That sort of thing.

It was an eye opener. In case someone else out there is looking for a hole-up spot, here is a glossary of terms for those looking for New Mexico rural real estate. These are key words and phrases found in actual land ads, and what they really mean.

If wide open spaces and sweeping desert panoramas are your cup of tea, then you may want to bag this one!

(The last human being to actually see this acre was a prospector in 1936 who was looking for the great scorpion graveyard. There is no record of him actually finding the graveyard, but he at least had the good manners to die in the attempt.)

Use your imagination with this choice piece of the planet, and see what you can come up with!

(Heaven knows the guy who owns this place now has scratched his head over what to do with it for years, and the only thing that keeps coming to him is the word "Sell.")

This precious parcel is just the place to find peace and quiet in your daily life.

(This place is so far off the grid the navigation satellites can't find it. The only radio station you can get on the portable out there is that big boomer that comes from the Navajo Nation, and then only when it rains.)

This corner of Heaven shows off Nature at its most impressive.

(The tornado that came through here blasted the barbed wire into a spider web those ranchers are still trying to untangle.)

Heavily treed.

(Well yes, if you consider 40 acres of cholla cactus a forest. It gives plenty of shade to the rattlesnakes, of course.)

Open to the fresh air of rural New Mexico!

(During my visit, the fresh air of rural New Mexico was rolling rocks the size of television sets along the arroyos.)

Untrammeled vistas!

(Never having trammeled a single vista, I wasn't sure what this meant. But Mr. Webster says a trammel is an impediment to free action. Now that definition made sense, but then he messed it up by saying it could also mean a contrivance hung in a fireplace to suspend pots and kettles. Flipped a coin. Impediments won. There was certainly nothing there to impede anything else.)

Stop at the store and ask directions.

(The locals always need a good laugh. Just don't be surprised, after driving four hours across New Mexico, to have someone look you in the eye and tell you that the only way to get there is to be born there.)

Could use some paint.

(Oh, I don't know about that, really. Hey, it could be that garbage-o-flage will be in vogue any day now, and at least it helps the place blend in with the neighborhood.)

Reach out and touch a bit of the history of the Old West!

(Billy the Kid shot someone about 20 miles down the road once.)

Just be sure to check with local regulations before planning your home on this lot.

(That's because it's in the bottom of an arroyo that averages four flash floods a year, and the county won't even let you picnic there.)

It's frustrating. Just once, wouldn't it be refreshing to read an honest real estate ad. Something like "An acre in the middle of nowhere with nothing but the wind to keep you company. Cheap, and worth every dollar. If you don't mind being alone, call me up." A guy might find a hole-up spot that way.

Enterprising Edibles

Dishes with a New Mexico twist

We need to design our own New Mexico fruits and vegetables in order to take our proper place in the world. Oh sure, you'll say, there's the chile. We're famous for it. Without chile, Hatch would just be a little door on a submarine. True, but not everyone in the world loves chile the way we do. For instance, Canadians think ketchup is too hot to handle and wouldn't last a minute in our best restaurants.

Since all fruits and vegetables have names, and since we have a hard time growing very many of those here anyway, what we need are some new fruits, some new vegetables and we get those by crossing known varieties until we achieve what we're after.

For example, Olallie State Park in Washington has been hanging around, looking pretty, for many years, but it wasn't until the invention of the Olallieberry that the state park took center stage in the world's eye. And how did they make an Olallieberry? By crossing the Loganberry with the Youngberry. In fact, the Youngberry itself is a cross between the Phenomenalberry and the dewberry. Indeed, those tricky rain forest types went a step further and crossed the Olallieberry with the blackberry and came up with the marionberry. This new fruit swept the nation with such fervor that they named a famous big-city mayor after it.

So it's overdue for New Mexico to stand up, grab its pollinating equipment and thrust itself into the front ranks of history by creating some new, strictly New Mexican edibles.

We should at least be able to outdo South Africa, which gave the world the *Passiflora edulis flavicarpa*. It is described thusly: "The aroma is less acidic than edulis and like *P. actinia* it has a hint of kerosene. Delicious." In addition to that, this plant looks like someone dumped scrambled eggs inside a soccer ball. The field is wide open for some New Mexico entries.

Naturally, we have a few suggestions.

Since we want these new fruits and vegetables to scream "New Mexico!" our choices are probably rather limited, but we should be able to come up with some, such as crossing wormwood and dill pickles to give us an "abiquiucumber."

PIE TOWN
PIÑON PEACHES

Strangely Nutty—
Totally Fruity!

Maudie Bell's
Blue Ribbon Winning
Piñon Peach Pies
$1.00

Roy's Top o' the World
Tomatoes
5 gallon bucket $1.00

PIE
TOWN
1 Mile

MEXico

In honor of a famous historic New Mexico rancher and politician, Albert Fall, we can combine the genes of an umbrella tree, orange pekoe and marijuana, giving us a real teapot dome.

To publicize the glories of our largest city, geneticists should be able to cross the best of Granny Smiths with chocolate chips to arrive at an "apple cookie." They would have to be harvested in early spring, though, to prevent melting the chocolate.

Bell peppers crossed with the flax plant would give us a spicy combo called "bell-lin," of course, and you could also spin it into cloth for a sizzling hot Saturday night ensemble.

For a hot drink, how about combining the cacao bean with hot milk, letting it age for a thousand years, and then quaff a "chaco-latte?"

Down along the Río Grande, in the heart of Albuquerque, we could cross Elbertas with the nettle bush, giving us the "tingley peach."

We should be able to market a fast-growing kind of guacamole by using the genes of the cottonwood to give us an "alamo-cado." But such a gene splice may not work in an arid region, so we could cross a nut tree with a coyote melon to give us an "almond-gourd-o."

And our New Mexico plant list wouldn't be complete without a three-way cross between a small tree fruit, some pinto beans and wild strawberries. We could call it "fruit or concert quinces."

The possibilities to promote our beautiful state are endless, but we must be careful to avoid the fate of that most famous of plant geneticists, Luther Burbank, who died while attempting to cross a busy street with a baby carriage.

It's an Instinct Thing

Humans drawn to fire, porch and knife

Somewhere deep within us lie instincts best understood by Charles Darwin. This month is when we gather for a time of gratitude, but also for an annual check-up, an evaluation of who and what we've become. And it usually happens with the family sitting around the fire. For some, the fire will be in deer camp next to a creek, but for most, the fire will be in a fireplace in our main rooms. We love it.

Naturally, it makes no sense at all.

Our brains have completely overridden our needs, in this case. Today's architects and builders can give us a house so well insulated that every time we light a candle, the temperature goes up 10 degrees. We can put so many poly-whatchits between us and a cold wind that a chill doesn't have a prayer. Our furnaces come on automatically and quietly and keep us at a boring 70 degrees, or maybe 68 if we're trying to save the planet.

So what do we do? We take this hermetically sealed cozy home and cut a hole in it so we can have a fire.

Makes no sense at all.

But in a way, it does. We have had fires in our homes for a lot longer than we've had poly-what-chamacallits. From the time our ancestors first learned to use it, the fire has come to mean the center of our very existence. Some of our ancestors worshipped it, but all of them used it. It gave us heat in the cold of winter, and cooked food. It kept away wild animals. It came to be our family's core, the symbol of home.

Despite Bic flicking and endless variations of no-match fire starters in outdoor catalogs, we insist on starting a campfire with a match. And the most respected outdoorsmen are the ones who can do it with a single match, in the rain. Why? Because those are the guys whose skills may mean the difference between life and death someday, and we want to hang around with them. Bics can run out of fuel. Skills last forever.

We practice doing it ourselves, from the time we're children, so we can take "home" with us wherever we go. When we're in the field, we have waterproof matches in our fanny packs and survival kits. There are matches in every emergency kit in every boat at sea. Stop and think about that one for a minute. There's a reason for the phrase "hearth and home," and the two are basically synonymous. A house with a fireplace, against all reason, is more valuable than one without. There are things we need in a home, and things we want. We want a fireplace, but seldom stop to wonder why.

And a porch. Give us a porch on the house, and go ahead and tack on a few thousand to the price. We want that porch. We want to be able to stand, with the fire in the fireplace at our backs, and look out at the rain, the snow, the uncertainties of the world from the shelter of the entrance to our cave, er ... that is, home, of course.

A porch is the buffer zone, the transition between the challenge of life and the comfort of home. On the porch we can plan our assault on the day while still having the feeling of being home.

And it's a great place to store firewood. These instincts we have are fascinating. Try an experiment someday. Stop any 10 men in business suits on the streets of a city and ask if you can sharpen your pencil with their pocketknife. I'll bet at least seven of them are carrying some little silly penknife of some kind. Why? Never mind that the knife isn't sharp enough to spread peanut butter. The truth is, despite its lack of size and effectiveness, with that pocketknife, we're armed.

With a pocketknife, a porch and a fireplace, we're true human beings. We can sit and whittle, and stay warm, and look out at the world from our own personal vantage point. Our fireplace may be a space in open desert between several rocks, or it may be a hearth surrounded by marble in a penthouse. Somehow, it doesn't seem to matter when we add things up. We can all look in the coals of the fire at the end of day and find answers to questions we didn't even know we had.

Not a bad deal.

Take the Test

Are you a real New Mexican?

Many people claim to be official New Mexicans, even if they haven't lived here that long, so we thought an exam might separate the wannabes from the real ones. Are you up to it?
Let's see how you do.

1. IN NEW MEXICO, THE FINAL HARD FROST OF THE YEAR OCCURS:
A. In early April.
B. Just before the coconuts ripen.
C. Two days after you shear 10,000 sheep.

2. A TWISTER ON THE PLAINS OF EASTERN NEW MEXICO IS ALSO KNOWN AS:
A. A tornado.
B. A whirlwind.
C. Urban renewal.

3. TOURIST SEASON IN NEW MEXICO MEANS:
A. Winter, when it is cold other places.
B. Summer, when it is hot other places.
C. A limit of one per hunter.

4. PETROGLYPHS IN NEW MEXICO CAN BEST BE DESCRIBED AS:
A. Pictures scratched on rocks by ancient peoples.
B. A store in Old Town selling Russian postcards.
C. The new brand of unleaded down at the gas station.

5. BROWN BAGGING IT IN NEW MEXICO CAN BEST BE DESCRIBED AS:
A. A clever way to shorten lunch hour.
B. An old method of cleaning out the fridge.
C. A head start on Christmas decorations.

6. IN NEW MEXICO A CANDLELIGHT VIGIL IS:
A. A way to pray for the dying.
B. Peaceful form of political demonstration.
C. What the Vigil family does during a power outage.

7. AT CHRISTMAS, LITTLE LUNCH BAGS WITH SAND AND CANDLES IN THEM ARE KNOWN AS:
A. Farolitos north of Albuquerque.
B. Luminarias from Albuquerque on south.
C. Little lunch bags with sand and candles in them everywhere else.

8. IN NEW MEXICO, RATTLESNAKES ARE BETTER KNOWN AS:

A. Rattlers.

B. Diamondbacks.

C. Our answer to the population explosion.

9. PEOPLE WHO LIVE IN MOBILE HOMES IN NEW MEXICO PLACE TIRES ON THE ROOF SO THEY CAN:

A. Play tic-tac-toe with the neighbors.

B. Have a place to hide Christmas presents.

C. Be ready to drive off in case the spring winds turn the mobile home over.

10. THE ANNUAL AVERAGE OF 9 INCHES OF RAINFALL IN NEW MEXICO:

A. Is far below the national average.

B. Gives new life to our beautiful forests and grass-lands.

C. Happens in about 45 minutes in July.

11. IN ALL NEW MEXICO HISTORY, THE BEST KNOWN NEW MEXICAN WAS:

A. Lucien Maxwell, the largest landowner in the history of the United States, who introduced public schools, public roads and banking to the territory.

B. Kit Carson, who blazed trails for the expeditions of John C. Fremont and ended the Confederate occupation of New Mexico during the Civil War.

C. Billy the Kid.

12. IN SANTA FE, THE MOST POPULAR FOOD IS:

A. Anything with green chile on it.

B. Anything with red chile on it.

C. Anything invented in Europe.

13. THE LOUDEST SOUND EVER HEARD IN NEW MEXICO OCCURRED WHEN:

A. The Jémez volcano erupted a million years ago sending ash around the world.

B. The first atomic bomb exploded at White Sands in 1945.

C. The University of New Mexico Lobos won a football game.

14. THE MOST TALENTED ARTIST IN THE HISTORY OF ALL NEW MEXICO IS:

A. Georgia O'Keeffe.

B. Peter Hurd.

C. You.

Let's see how you did. Every time you answered C., give yourself 10 points. For every B., five points. For every A., you must send beer to the cowboys of New Mexico.

If you scored 90-100, you are a real New Mexican. If you scored 50-90, you've been study-ing, but haven't been here long enough yet. Spend more time here and take the test again. If you scored less than 50, you've been reading guide-books but have yet to leave New Jersey. If you think keeping score is silly, you're right.

70

Physics Folly

Theory of Relativity with a family twist

As fall falls on us with its blend of Halloween colors, the filigree lace of tree branches against an autumn sky, and the anticipation of leftover trick-or-treat candy, our thoughts naturally turn to physics. At least that's how things are here on the porch in company with a bluetick hound and an adult beverage.

A long time ago now, a guy with a great moustache and hair that wouldn't stay combed coined what he called "The Theory of Relativity." It had something to do with mass, energy and the speed of light, and he was able to pull this off because he was the only one who knew what he was talking about. He got to be famous over that, though, and they named some bagels after him.

But, hey, how long ago was that? We're past due for an updated theory of relativity, and that's why we're here on the porch, after all. We never were as strong as we used to be any more, but like any handicap, that just sharpened the brain to the point of downright embarrassment.

So here's the "Theory of Relativity, P.I." (Porch Improved): G=N*DIF.

For those of who aren't blessed with an honorary diploma from Owens Valley High School, allow me to translate. In layman's terms, it reads: "Greed equals the need multiplied by the distance in the family."

You're welcome.

This formula was not arrived at haphazardly, but only after several hours of cosmic contemplation and beverage sipping. To explain how this works, all we need to do is study the relationships in a family. Would you borrow a shovel from your wife? No, of course not. If a guy didn't have access to his own shovel, he'd never hear the end of it, from his wife or from any of the guys at the feed store who heard about it. That kind of deal just doesn't work when it's that close to home.

So do you borrow that shovel from your brother? Again, the word will spread within the family, and they'll all nod their heads knowingly, thinking silently all the while, "We all knew he'd come to this.

He has grandchildren, for Pete's sake, and can't afford a shovel."

So what we want to do here is skip several degrees of relationship until we find just the guy we need: perhaps our sister-in-law's cousin. With him we have a double bonus going for us, because he is far enough removed from the family to actually have enough money to own a shovel, and he is also far enough removed that if he calls us names and reviles us for our penury, we don't care. It's a double blessing, thanks to the Theory of Relativity, P.I.

But, you say (astute observer that you are), the T. of R., P.I. says you multiply the need times the distance in the family, right? Of course. That's why we're not simply going to hit him up for use of the shovel but plan also to wheedle and whine until he comes over with that new front-end loader and does the digging for us, too. Taking it to its logical far-out conclusion, if this sister-in-law's cousin had an uncle with a half brother, we could hit that half brother up for all the dirt moving and lunch besides!

That's the genius of this updated theory of relativity. The more removed the relative is, the more likely he is to be well fixed and the greedier you are allowed to be.

Let's face it—it's really only the immediate family we care about. The ones we have to face at Thanksgiving. When we start branching off into distant cousins and aunts once removed, it should be for a good reason. That's why it's always good to do your homework before putting the T. of R., P.I. into practice. Learn something about this distant relative that you can use as a lever to open the goody jar. For example, you could smile, introduce yourself as kinfolks, and say, "I understand you're a citizen of the United States. What a coincidence!"

Then, after the two of you have compared the Fourth Amendment with the findings of the Continental Congress, you can make your pitch for that Chevy pickup of his.

But things don't always work out the way you hope. For example, even after considerable family research, I've failed to put Bill Gates even on the fringes of my relativity. Oh well, no one said physics was perfect.

WINTER

Going Dutch

A prize-winning cobbler in 18 minutes

L eave it to Ed Parsons to become an instant legend in Texas. Ed runs a trucking company here in New Mexico for his daily bread. But for his passion, Ed is just about the best Dutch oven cook … period.

And there he was, a few years ago now, the only out-of-state chuck-wagon owner and Dutch oven cook among hundreds of Texans somewhere down where the Río Grande takes a big bend.

It began when a reporter from a local newspaper went to cover the huge event, where hundreds of chuck wagons were set up, and hundreds of fires built, and there were hundreds of guys and gals standing around wearing riding boots, spurs and aprons. And there wasn't a horse in sight.

Naturally, when a reporter is wondering which of these bowlegged marvels to immortalize in print, someone from a foreign country (in this case, New Mexico) instantly comes to mind. And so it was that Ed was singled out for glory.

This Dutch oven cooking is really an art form—part science and part feel—and the reason some of us who have cooked in camps like it

is simple—it's very forgiving. If you're late coming back to camp, and you've had a roast buried in this heavy cast-iron pot all day, it really doesn't matter too much if you've been gone six hours or 12, the contents will still send hungry outdoorsmen into orbits of delight.

The reason for this is that the Dutch oven is heavy cast iron, seasoned on the inside so food won't stick, and it tends to heat slowly and evenly. With food that needs a thorough cooking, like bear and pork roasts (both carry the trichinosis parasite), a Dutch oven is just the thing. It is the ancestor of the electric Crock-Pot, but can be cooked easily over an open fire. The flames tend to mess up the wiring on a Crock-Pot.

There are so-called Dutch ovens that have glass lids, or iron lids that slope at the edges. These are for cooking in a range, not out on the range. They aren't real. They were designed for casseroles, so town cooks can pretend they are real camp cooks. It helps to play music from the Sons of the Pioneers while cooking that way.

But a real Dutch oven has legs under it and a

lid with a flange running around the outside to help hold coals in place. You can put coals under and on top of it, and adjust it so it bakes bread, cooks potatoes and carrots, makes pies, cakes, casseroles and just about anything else you want.

Some of us just shovel coals out of the cooking fire to do this. Others, those of a more scientific bent, use charcoal briquettes. Ed Parsons is one of those. He cooks for large parties of people and he wants to have everything just right, and all at the same time, so he uses the briquettes to make this almost error-proof.

He knows exactly how many briquettes to put under each Dutch oven and how many on top, and precisely how long it will take.

And with his prize-winning cobbler? "Eighteen minutes," he says. "Exactly 18 minutes."

Back to Texas and Ed starting his cobbler while the reporter talks to him. He glances slyly at his watch and then suggests they go somewhere quieter, where they can talk more easily. So he and the reporter walk about 100 yards away from the din of the chuck wagons and the radiated heat of the many cooking fires, and sit down and talk.

Exactly 18 minutes later, Parsons holds up a finger for silence, then sniffs the breeze.

"I have to get back," he tells her, "my cobbler is done. I can smell it."

"That's not possible!" she says, as there are maybe 15 other chuck wagons between them and his cobbler.

"A good cook can always tell his own cobbler," Ed says, sniffing again. "Yep, just turning golden brown on top."

And he walked back there with her, popped the top on the Dutch oven, and there was a perfect cobbler.

When that story appeared in the papers, New Mexican Dutch oven cooks, and Ed Parsons in particular, entered the realms of legend.

Slim's Dutch Oven Moose (or Elk, Deer or Beef) Roast

Warm a 12-inch Dutch oven. Place a 3-pound roast inside and braise it on both sides over the fire.

Then dig a hole and put coals in the bottom. Set the Dutch oven in the hole. Add to the roast 1/2 can of beer, a bunch of potatoes and carrots. Then cover with the lid, shovel more coals on the top, cover the top coals with a piece of metal of some sort, then pile dirt on the top of the metal.
Go away all day.

It'll start being ready about midafternoon, but if you don't get back until after dark, it'll still be ready.

Snow Appeal

White stuff stirs our winter juices

We here in the valleys look at the mountain heights with undisguised envy when a brisk morning shows a sprinkling of white on top.

Why is it that getting cold in the snow appeals to us so much?

If we spent our youth in Duluth, we're talking nostalgia here. Even though when we retired, we moved here so we didn't have to shovel snow anymore. Here in New Mexico, we discovered, we could create a lawn out of white rocks that never needs to be mowed, and never—never—have to shovel snow. But somehow that snow up there on the mountain reminds us, beckons us. Have we forgotten? Hey, this is a reminder that winter is going on somewhere, even if down here on Camino Gavacho it almost never touches the ground. Maybe that's why, even in retirement, we get in the car and drive up the canyon roads to look at it. We still need to touch base with our past and think on who and what we were.

If we spent our childhood in Hollywood, or a more tropical place than New Mexico, the appeal of snow high on the mountains is easy to figure. It's what we were denied. Despite being purebred, registered citizens of the United States of America, we were denied snow. We sang "Frosty the Snowman" thinking he was some alien that landed on a movie set.

We thought the movie *White Christmas* was probably something racist. We had to use rocks instead of snowballs in snowball fights. We were in trouble a lot. Snow was something that happened on television and three times a year on mountains more than 5,000 feet high, and we were stuck down in the palm trees singing Beach Boys songs. It wasn't fair. We didn't even know anyone who owned a sled. When, that one Saturday each winter, we talked our parents into driving us up to wallow around in 6 inches of sloppy, melting slush, we had only inner tubes to slide on. If we couldn't afford inner tubes, we came down the hill on a cousin.

Up in the mountains of New Mexico, people complain about the snow, but secretly they love the stuff. How do we know? Because it is more expensive to live in the mountains of New Mexico

than down in the valleys where it doesn't snow much. Ergo, therefore and forthwith, why spend more money to be miserable? Is that anything anyone would do willingly? That makes as much sense as actually trying to live in a big city.

So we patiently listen to the mountain folks complain about the snow and how long it takes them to shovel off their cedar deck, which they don't use this time of year anyway, and we smile to ourselves ... because we know. In their hearts they wouldn't embrace the valleys. They would pine for the pines until someone dragged them back up the mountain and returned them to their natural habitat.

If we spent our youth in Truth (or Consequences), we were largely cheated as well. But if our spouse is from Taos, at least she got to know snow. But no matter where we are from, there's something about snow that appeals to our seasonal sense of what's right.

It's a show that tells us the world is turning about as it should. It is a way of telling us that we can be glad we're down here where we don't have to shovel it, or we can reminisce on how much fun it used to be, or we can throw skis in the car and drive up to slide around in it. If we're truly diseased, we can make endless plans for someday living where it would snow on us regularly, blessing our being with the rich winter blanket.

And we know that once, or maybe even three times this winter, snow will touch our ground and our lives right down here in the valley. It always does. And each winter morning we awake with that anticipation and look out the window, hoping we can wake our loved ones by saying, "It's snowing."

Not so Perfect

Resolving your reputation a slam-dunk

The problem with making any New Year's resolutions is that I've done it for so many years now that I'm darn near perfect.

I began picking up my socks before the earth cooled completely, I start each day before the sun does, and I quit smoking my pipe when Reagan was president. While my nickname doesn't fit me quite as well as it used to, I'm also not losing any sleep over matters of obesity yet, either. I'm teaching myself to play a Chinese accordion, I haven't lied recently about how old I actually am and I learned enough French pronunciation to order a sandwich in Santa Fe. Yep. Darn near perfect.

But there are still those pesky resolutions to make, which will enable us to look forward to spring and to becoming even more sublime in every aspect. So maybe it's time to work on the reputation a little bit.

What kind of reputation? Well, without hamstringing the neighborhood, we can manage to be known for honesty and reliability. That's almost a slam-dunk. But when we're finally gone over that last ridge, how do we really want to be remembered? With laughter, of course. It is our jobs as parents to do whatever is in our power to embarrass our children and grandchildren by deviating just slightly from the norm. Just enough to make a total stranger ask himself, "Psychotic? Is he or isn't he?" We can now put ourselves on a list to let sales folks know not to call us at home, for example. But that would keep us from trying something more fun.

Let's resolve to answer the next sales call on the phone by saying, "Congratulations! By calling this number you have automatically qualified to be in a drawing for an all-expenses-paid trip to Lubbock, Texas, for the annual National Cowboy Symposium, and for a 10 percent discount on barbecue during your entire stay. Nothing further is required from you. You are automatically entered, and the nominal entry charge of $7.50 will be added to your regular phone bill under the heading of regulatory fees. Thank you for participating and good luck in the drawing." Click.

Let's also resolve (if we're over 40 years old) to learn at least one of those modern dance moves that looks as though we'd either been pole-axed or lost control of most bodily functions, and to then use that whenever our children or grandchildren have friends over to the house. If we should give a few of those moves in front of them every time the music was played a bit too loudly, the world would become a much quieter place.

One guy I heard of was visiting his daughter and her family in a small coastal town up north once, and decided to try out his new fly rod. The only problem was, the closest water (he was afoot) was the local small boat harbor in a quiet piece of Pacific Ocean.

This fellow discovered you could still practice casting trout flies, even if you knew you wouldn't catch anything but ridicule and had to dodge seagulls to do it. But his family was slightly on the horrified side, because it took only five minutes for the whole town to discover whose father this was, and there was speculation going around about certain conditions being hereditary. To save the day, this fisherman's daughter quietly carried two large Dolly Varden trout down to the ocean-front and slipped them to yon doddering dad when he was out of sight of the locals at the coffee shop. When he walked back up the beach with his fly rod, carrying two large freshwater fish, what had been a mere eccentricity surged dangerously close to legend.

On the only occasion I met actor Elliott Gould, he was wearing a tuxedo and ratty sneakers. It does tend to leave an impression.

Another inspiration of the past was the man who enjoyed driving in the country with his daughters and their friends. He was a musical sort—did quite a bit of church choir singing, things like that—so when he'd spy a turkey farm, he'd always pull over and stop.

"No!" cried the daughters. All in vain. With glee, he'd jump out of the car, look around on the ground for a likely sized stick, and tap softly on the fence to get the attention of the turkeys.

("What's your dad doing?" "No … Daddy don't do this… not today!")

When thousands of turkey necks were swiveled toward the barbed-wire podium, the conductor would raise both hands and tell the assembled feathered dinners, "All right, people, let's do the Brahms now. From the top. Sopranos ready? Tenors ready? White meat ready?

"Drumsticks? All right. Now let's start together."

With that, he would lean forward, wave the baton and yell "Gobble-gobble-gobble!" And from a thousand red crinkly throats would come an answering chorus of gobbles loud enough to usually bring an irate farmer out of the house. Some people, our conductor discovered, were more interested in weight than in harmony.

Someday, hopefully many years from now, we'll check out and our relatives and friends will get together and laugh about things we did and said. And wouldn't it be a shame if any of them had to lie?

84

Stinkin' Skunks
Maligned critters not on most popular list

He has a brain about the size of a marble, can't see very well and isn't very fast. No, he isn't on the city council, but we all know him. In fact, we can be aware of him while driving 65 miles an hour down the freeway hours after his visit.

He's our striped skunk, the No. 1 animal we won't invite to a party. If points were given for unpopularity, he'd win the Nobel Prize for ostracism. His smell can gag a sick dog off a gut truck, and that's before he sprays anything. The experts say Ol' Stripes can spray up to 15 feet. If that's true, how then can he empty a square city block with a single squirt?

He's not even popular in the animal family. The spotted skunk (who is no prize himself) doesn't claim kinship. Ol' Stripes is listed officially as *Mephitis mephitis*. Spotty clocks in as *Spirogale putorius*. The other varmint often associated with the striped skunk is the civet cat, which lives in Africa and Asia. But he's known in Latin as *Civettictis civetta*, which isn't even close to mephitis, either. Mephitis sounds a lot like Mephistopheles, doesn't it?

At least the civet cat contributes something to society. The Chinese eat him in a very popular soup, one that has that certain piquant *como se llama*, which just drives them wild as they reminisce out in the rice paddies. Not only that, but the civet cat contributes greatly to the rarest gourmet coffee in the world. It's known as Kopi Luwak coffee. Let us now bow our heads and quote:

"Kopi Luwak is so unusual that many people think it's a myth. On the island of Sumatra a small animal (civet cat) eats the coffee fruits and the seeds (beans) pass through its digestive system and (are) excreted. The beans are collected from the jungle floor and processed as normal coffee. The taste is supposedly much richer than typical coffee, with an almost chocolate undertone."

Whoa now! You know, Mavis, I believe I'll skip the refill this morning. Running late for work as it is. This might just be a clue as to why this coffee is so rare.

No one claims Ol' Stripes for a relative these days. Maybe back when giant sloths hung around

New Mexico, but if so, any cousins have since died of shame. Our striped skunk doesn't add a lot to our quality of life. Oh, as a plus, the ever-forgiving biologists point out that skunks eat grasshoppers.

Well, so do trout, and it's a lot more fun trying to get a trout to eat one. Besides grasshoppers, skunks enjoy canned sardines, peanut butter and marshmallows. They carry rabies, stay out all night, live under the house and smell bad. Had a cousin like that.

If skunks move under your house, they can be easily discouraged from returning by—get this—using an unpleasant odor as a repellent. That's right. Roll a handful of mothballs under the house and the problem is solved. They can't stand the smell of naphthalene.

And, if worse comes to worst and Poochie should end up with a face full of skunk stink, forget the tomato juice. Here's a tip from Doc Minter up in the Jémez Mountains. Smear said mutt with a mixture of one quart of hydrogen peroxide, one teaspoon of liquid detergent and a quarter cup of baking soda. Don't get it in his eyes.

Skunk stink can wilt saltine crackers when they're still sealed, evacuate neighbors faster than a forest fire and topple Third World governments. You have to admire professionalism wherever you find it.

Ah, Mephitis, me lad! You may be gone from our sight, but the memory lingers on.

Slingin' Mud

By jingo, New Mexicans get down and dirty with adobe

Mientras que descansas, has adobes. (While you rest, make adobes.)

Building a house of adobe brick is like beating your head against a wall; it feels so good when you stop.

But we love our mud houses. We get messy. We get dirty. We get slipped discs. But we love our mud houses.

It makes no sense at all to build a house out of mud. If the roof fails, the living room becomes a large brown lump wrapped around a coffee table. An adobe house has all the insulating qualities of a sheet of onion-skin paper. The bricks weigh more than your left leg. Each. But we love our mud houses.

An adobe house is dangerous in earthquake zones. You can't build one in California, for example. But we don't have earthquakes here, and we love our mud houses.

Building an adobe house takes so many hours of hard labor that only the very rich or the very unemployed can afford one. Maybe that's one reason we love them so much. Build one and let the neighbors guess whether you're rich or broke. But we do love them, these mud houses of ours.

Why? Because we have a reverence for tradition that defies common sense. It may be harder, it may be more expensive, it may be physically painful, but by jingo, it's our way and we'll change our minds only when they pry the adobe forms from our cold, dead fingers.

Let's face it, there are things we do just because we live here. We pour spicy red sauce on our scrambled eggs. We build a giant statue in Santa Fe each year just to burn it down. If we could catch coyotes, we'd tie bandannas around their necks just to embarrass them. We prefer wearing jewelry made of blue rocks. Just because we live here.

And just because we live here, we like to live in mud houses.

It's been that way since the Spanish introduced sun-dried mud bricks to the New World. Before that, the Pueblo Indians built out of cut sod, called *terrones*.

These houses also tended to dissolve after a leak in the roof, but at least the occupants had interesting grass root patterns to look at.

The Spanish called their sun-dried bricks "adobe," which loosely translates as "my back hurts."

But adobe houses are cool in summer and warm in winter. Everyone knows that. This is due to a wall several feet thick made of dried mud and weighing slightly more than New Jersey having what is known as "mass."

Since the insulation R-value of an adobe brick has a decimal point to the left of it, the wall makes up for it by being big and heavy.

Adobe proponents are quick to point out that the mass of the walls keeps the summer sun from heating up the house until about 8 p.m., when the heat finally breaches the last layer of mud and makes it possible to bake bread on the TV set. Sleeping, of course, is out of the question, but beer helps.

Likewise, in winter it stays nice and warm ... unless the fire goes out.

But we gladly take all that abuse and laugh—Ha!—in the face of reason. We are people of the earth and our homes grow organically from the very soil itself. Building with adobe, you see, is holistic, is natural, is painful.

Don't bother us with facts.

We love our mud houses.

What a Concept

Art is whatever you say it is

As honorary chairman of the smallest minority in New Mexico, (Certifiable Non-Artists of Enchantment)—just because I couldn't draw fire in Afghanistan—I've always felt left out.

"But," well-meaning friends say, "you draw pictures with your words."

Even though that's hooey, still it gave me an idea, because I believe the secret to being a successful artist is not just in being able to paint something, but also by being able to name it something no one else can figure out.

The really brave artists are those who name their paintings *Cottonwoods in Autumn,* because then people expect certain shapes and colors. But let's say you march to that different drummer and see shapes and colors that haven't been seen since the last time beer was free. What then?

Then you paint whatever you want, and use your creative energy in naming the work so no one else knows what to expect.

For example, paint something, then give it a name from the multiple choices below.

The (intimacy, fragrance, shame, triumph, defloration, depilation, degradation, exaltation, putrescence, challenge, immersion, emersion, subversion, flagellation, pasteurization) of (innocence, cowardice, gentility, pubescence, aggression, ferocity, animosity, escalation, totality, penstemons, Santa Fe, rigor mortis, ebullience, sanguinity, virginity, branch water, flapdoodle).

These simple suggestions above give a new artist 255 possible titles for a work of art. You're welcome. Now you can concentrate on the important things, like painting something that would fit one of those titles.

I can't wait to see *The Aggression of Penstemons* and *The Subversion of Depilation.*

Then there are the "collection" titles, which have enjoyed a loyal following lately. These would be excellent titles for paintings that have more than one thing in them. It would be up to the artist, of course, to decide which objects to paint more than one of. The smart ones usually pick something they can paint well.

But these titles have to sport that same ethereal, airy-fairy quality, too, or someone might tie you down to it.

For example, if you have a painting called *A Gathering of Lizards,* there's always someone who will look at it and say, "I've seen lizards gather, and that don't look like it."

So, to avoid being pinned down, you need titles more like the following:

A (borrowing, constellation, coagulation, parturition, cycle, massing, congregation, round-up, pot full, effervescence, powdering, whole slug, miscellany, cotillion, sprinkling, bouquet, corralling, kenneling, magnificence) of (extrusions, simulations, conclusions, retribution, delight, pulchritude, synchronism, meeblies, salutations, protuberance, vascularity, spontaneity, globalism).

If someone viewing your painting should mention that *meeblies* isn't an actual word in English, just say, "Concepts take over where mere words fail us."

If an art fan should say that a title like *A Kenneling of Spontaneity* doesn't make sense, here's how to respond.

1. Tip your glasses down to the tip of your nose so you can stare over them. If you don't normally wear glasses, borrow some.

2. Ask this person, "Are you perhaps the art critic for the *Socorro Defensor Chieftain?*" 'Why, no,' they'll say, then,

3. Smirk slightly and say, "I thought not."

You have two essential things going for you: Namely, art is whatever you say it is, and everyone knows artists are people of vision and should never be questioned. It's that beautiful mystique that all true artists carry in their portfolios. The outside world looks at them and thinks they have an inside track to the meaning of life. This has undoubtedly saved a great deal of embarrassment over the centuries, and has also saved art galleries from disintegrating from too much laughter.

If your eye is toward the mountain and the canvas, if your mind sees the solutions to complicated math problems through color and shape, if you are able to cough up enough money for some paint and canvas, New Mexico is your oyster.

But you must always be very careful not to give away the fact that you're normal. That might ruin the tourist trade.

Waiting for the Nobel

Chances seem slim for guy named Slim

When the awful news came, it hit me like a week with two Mondays. For days afterward I moped around, refusing to eat the food in my dish, bereft of smiling countenance. The news couldn't have been worse; for the 64th year in a row—64 years, mind you—I didn't win the Nobel Prize for literature. And I'm danged tired of it.

What do they want, for Pete's sake? Haven't I given them enough Porch columns yet to constitute a life's legacy of literature? Haven't they read my books ... dadgummed classics, too (meaning out of print) like *Dogsled, A True Tale of the North*? What's a guy have to do to get their attention?

The Nobel, you see, is the biggie. The Pulitzer is wonderful, of course. You can win a Pulitzer for a single bit of writing. I'm still working on my first one of those at the minute, too. But the Nobel? That one puts the cherry on the total brouhaha of a life's work.

You know the story behind it, of course. You've heard of Alfred Nobel, who invented dynamite, and then made so much money on it he offered to give a bunch of it each year to someone who could figure out how not to use his product. This was called the Nobel Peace Prize. Then, to prevent being called a one-trick pony, they expanded the monetary awards to include physics, medicine, mathematics, literature and fence building.

For years now, the Nobel Prize for literature has loomed as a writing cowboy's biggest trophy buckle. They give you a bunch of prize money, too, and you get to go to Sweden and eat meatballs and wear a tuxedo and meet blond people and say, "Ya, sure." And the whole thing's on the house.

Maybe I'm just going about this Nobel Prize stuff all wrong. I used to think, "Hey, all I have to do is just sit here and write good stuff and they'll call me up and say come get your money." But after being overlooked year after year, I got to thinking maybe that isn't the way to handle things. So I looked up past winners to see if I could find some common threads winding through their lives.

Boy, was I right! In the first place, to be in contention for the Nobel Prize, you should start with an unpronounceable name: like Imre Kertesz,

V.S. Naipaul, Gao Xingjian, Wislawa Szymborska, Kenzaburo Oe, Naguib Mahfouz, Wole Soyinka and Rabindranath Tagore.

Slim is just too easy to pronounce, and that may be a huge strike against me. Picture the Nobel judges, getting ready to pick a winner. Just like in Santa Fe, where food is prized more for its unpronounceability than its taste—like baba ganouj, ratatouille and arugula—maybe they pick laureates by the difficulty in pronouncing their names. Makes sense. For one thing, who's going to check up on you? No one is likely to say, "That Wislawa Szymborska is OK. I've read all her stuff, but she does tend to split infinitives." No. The cognoscenti (Latin for "those who knowingly smell") will just nod silently, as though in wisdom. The one-line reason for Szymborska's prize is this: "for poetry that with ironic precision allows the historical and biological context to come to light in fragments of human reality."

Hell, we do that every month right here in this space.

I also saw that most Nobel laureates for literature come from places where people struggle with the English language. Well, my cabin is smack in the middle of New Mexico, but do you think I score any points for that?

Then I checked to see which Americans had won, and that was the crusher. That was the real eye opener. The coup d'état. The silver bullet. There before me lay the real reason the Swedish judges pass me by year after literary year. Among the Americans who have eaten the meatballs and gotten the free trip were John Steinbeck, Ernest Hemingway, William Faulkner, Eugene O'Neill and Sinclair Lewis.

I'm doomed. There's just no way I can drink that much.